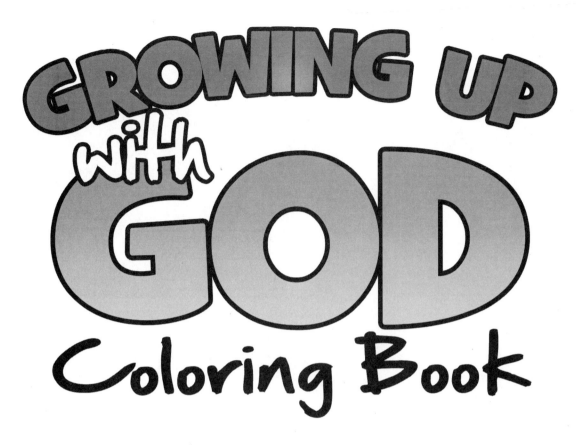

GROWING UP with GOD
Coloring Book

SHAWN BOLZ

ISBN: 978-1-942306-75-7

Illustrations | R.W. Lamont Hunt | www.dakotakidcreations.com

Cover design | Yvonne Parks | www.pearcreative.ca

The Growing Up with God friends are at summer camp.

Lucas is helping Maria to believe she can hear from God.

While Maria is hearing from God about her destiny,
Hartley knows her destiny is s'mores!

Maria shares with her friends that God showed
her she would be an actress.

Lucas is excited to be back home from camp.

Lucas tells his mom all about the games, fun, and what God did.

Lucas shares how someone gave him a prophecy about growing in compassion.

That night, Lucas prays for his words to come true.

There is no room for Maria in acting class at her community theater.

Harper's mom calls Maria's mom and invites Maria to join
kids' choir at the theater instead.

Maria, Harper, Lucas, and Jarvis are praying together on social media, practicing sharing God's heart with each other.

Maria hears something from God for Lucas's grandma
She goes to bed knowing God will fulfill her promise too!

Soccer is Lucas's life!

A new kid, Jamal, gets pushed down by a bully.

Lucas tries to help Jamal up, but the bully pushes Lucas down onto Jamal.

Jamal is sad, but Lucas makes friends with him.

Maria finds out her choir class is going to perform a musical and is so excited!

Maria tries out for the very professional Mr. Wright from Broadway.

There is a girl in class named Brooke who is the best out of everyone.

Maria is sad that Brooke is a better singer, but God tells her that her destiny is to love everyone involved in entertainment—people like Brooke.

Jamal and Lucas are going to hang out with Lucas's dad after soccer practice.

Lucas and Jamal have pizza, play video games, and Lucas wins a
stuffed toy that looks just like Jarvis.

Jamal shares he has had a hard life and is a foster kid.
Lucas has true compassion.

Lucas's parents explain how to love Jamal and see him in God's fullness.

Maria wants the main role in the musical and can't think
about anything else.

Maria and Harper are excited to audition! Brooke is sick and can't try out.

Maria feels bad and wants to pray for Brooke to be healed,
because loving Brooke is her destiny.

Brooke is healed! She auditions and gets the part.
Harper is so proud of Maria

The kids are going to play after school at Maria's house.

The school bully, Jeffrey, picks on Jamal and the other kids,
but Lucas has a talk with him.

Jeffrey agrees to stop bullying Jamal and they drive off, finally at peace.

Lucas's parents ask him if he would think about their family
adopting Jamal! Lucas is so happy.

Brooke is praying that God will show her the perfect outfit for an audition.

Maria and Harper explain that God doesn't always speak about things because he loves to give us the power to make great decisions. Brooke chooses her outfit.

The girls go to her audition with her, but when they meet
the casting director, he wants all three of them to try out!

The casting director casts them all in a real commercial.
Maria's word from God begins to be fulfilled about being an actress.

The kids are all in Sunday school learning about growing up
with God in friendship.

The children's pastor says that the Holy Spirit helps us to know God's heart, just like a friend knows our heart. Harper and Maria feel that closeness in their friendship.

Jamal is impacted by the message on friendship with God, and he can see how Lucas has shown him that kind of friendship.

Jamal wants to ask Jesus into his heart. The kids all pray with him!

Lucas and Maria tell Brooke and Jamal about what God told them last year at summer camp. They explain that Brooke and Jamal were the people God used to teach them about their callings and destinies of acting and compassion.

GROWING UP WITH GOD
Chapter Book

Join Lucas and Maria and friends on their everyday adventures in friendship with God!

Lucas knows God talks to him, but he would have never imagined that he would hear such a specific thing about his year . . . and could Maria really have heard God about her destiny? They both have to wonder if God speaks to kids this way. Over the months that follow, God begins to connect them to other kids that grow into friends. Who could have guessed that by the end of the year, their lives would be so exciting!

Award-winning illustrator Lamont Hunt illustrates the rich, vibrant God journey of kids you can relate to. By best-selling author Shawn Bolz.

Growing Up with God is an amazing adventure!

growingupwithgod.com

GROWING UP WITH GOD
Workbook

An accompaniment for *Growing Up with God*, the children's chapter book, this workbook will encourage your kids to practice hearing God's voice.

Not only does this workbook teach children how to listen to God, it also gives them the tools they need to support and believe in themselves and each other.

In each section that relates to a chapter in *Growing Up with God*, your children will find:

- A reminder of what was in the chapter
- A true story from a kid their age about how he or she encountered God
- Three important things to know about God's voice
- Bible verses to back up the teaching
- Questions for them to think about and answer
- A prayer
- Illustrations from the book to keep the content focused & exciting

This generation of kids will be the most powerful, prophetic generation yet, and this workbook is a journal and guide will help them fulfill that destiny.

GROWING UP WITH GOD
Study Course

Equip future generations with the life-changing tools
they need to grow into all God has for them.

**CHAPTER BOOK | WORKBOOK | COLORING BOOK
TEACHER'S GUIDE | 10 DVD SESSIONS**

  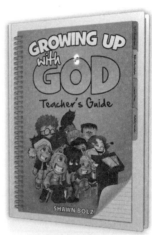 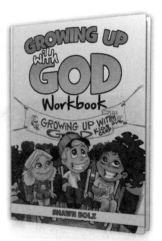

Ideal for use in Sunday school, VBS,
small groups, and homeschool settings.

Parent tips included in each chapter!